WHEN IT'S TIME®

LEADER'S GUIDE

Leading Your Group
Through End-of-Life Pre-Planning
and Survivor Support

RICK CRAIG

Bella Matt Press

When It's Time®
Bella Matt Press
www.whenitstime.org

Due to the changing nature of the internet, any web address, links, or URLs listed in this book may have been altered and may no longer be accessible.

Cover Photo: Shawn Montoya
Design: Sarah Barnum | www.trailblazes.com
Author photo: Lea Dawn Photography

ISBN
Printed in the United States of America

Scripture is clear about serving others,
and I have found tremendous joy
in serving people preparing for
end-of-life or survivors learning a
new rhythm of life.

As a facilitator, you have the
opportunity to help others learn how to prepare
for one of the most challenging days
of their life—facing death or becoming a survivor.

Your investment into becoming a
facilitator of this material will change
peoples' lives.

CONTENTS

PART TWO
Building Your End-of-Life Plan

FOREWORD

I vividly remember the day I met my friend Rick Craig. He had been invited to speak at our church after writing his first book, *When It's Time*®. Our pastor introduced Rick as an expert on a subject everyone needs to hear about, but few are eager to discuss—end-of-life planning. As a licensed funeral director who has counseled countless families both in moments of need and in preparation for it, I am deeply aware of the profound difference planning ahead makes for survivors. The experience for the family can be as stark as night and day.

Over a decade ago, I transitioned from the funeral profession to healthcare as an educator with an organ procurement organization. A significant part of my role is teaching about the end-of-life decision to become an organ, eye, and tissue donor. Ideally, your loved ones should hear about your decision long before the need arises, not for the first time at the hospital. When I heard Rick speak about his book, I knew I needed a copy. Once I started reading, it quickly became clear that Rick and I shared a like-minded approach to planning for the inevitable.

Rick's expertise extends far beyond textbook knowledge; it is deeply rooted in his personal experience with loss. He knows firsthand the importance of planning properly and receiving accurate information from a reliable source. When it comes to death and dying, there is only one chance to get it right. Over time, I've also come to know Rick as a teacher at heart. After his book, he created a companion workbook and now offers this resource to train others in teaching end-of-life planning. If you wish to equip people in your community to prepare for life's final chapter, this leader's guide is invaluable.

The material in this guide is also an essential resource for those who have experienced sudden or unexpected loss. Walking alongside someone who has recently lost a loved one is an incredible honor, and attending a class based on Rick Craig's *When It's Time®* will equip you to support the bereaved more effectively. Whether for at-need care or advance planning, this facilitator training proves beneficial. Of particular importance is Part Two, which guides you, the future expert, through the process of getting your own affairs in order. After all, you cannot teach what you haven't personally experienced. Sharing from your own experience, rather than relying on theoretical knowledge, will resonate more deeply with your students.

No matter your stage in life, having your affairs in order brings a tremendous sense of relief. While no one enjoys contemplating their own death, taking the time to follow Rick's suggestions is time well spent. Once your plans are complete, be sure to communicate your wishes to your family and let them know where they can access the necessary information. After that, you can set the matter aside and focus on enjoying life. Each day is a gift from God and should be lived accordingly.

Christopher Donhost
Former Chairman of Donate Life America's
Funeral Services Committee

ABOUT THE AUTHOR

Pastor Rick Craig was a coach for the small-group ministry at a church with a membership of over 2,000, and then a pastor of small groups with over a 70 percent participation rate of the church body. In addition, Rick has written training guides for leaders and facilitated seminars on how to be a leader of small groups. Rick is the author of *When It's Time® End-of-Planning at Any Age; Make it Part of Your Legacy* and *When It's Time® An End-of-Life Workbook for Pre-Planners and Survivors.*

As a pastor who frequently officiates funeral and memorial services for retired military, law enforcement officers, and civilians, his ability to connect with survivors and assist them on their journey of beginning a new rhythm of life has been invaluable. Sharing his knowledge through webinars, podcasts, and seminars, he equips pre-planners to begin or complete their plans as an act of love for their survivors. You, too, can add to your legacy with a well-thought-out plan.

Connect with Rick:
www.whenitstime.org
pastorrickcraig@whenitstime.org
Find his books on Amazon

PREFACE

Greetings, Group Leader.

Taking on the role of leader carries responsibilities and rewards. I have learned through my years of being a group member, apprentice leader, co-leader, leader, small-group coach, small-group pastor, and now an author and trainer, how extremely satisfying it can be to witness someone be called into leadership and succeed. Part of any good leader's legacy is participants who grow by making course corrections to live better. Everyone wins when that happens!

Our team at Pastor Rick Craig Ministries is dedicated to helping you become a leader who influences group members to be more intentional, live life more abundantly, and author legacies for their survivors.

I highly encourage you to take this journey of leadership with a co-leader so you can support one another, learn from one another, and partner with one another to develop a game plan to replicate yourselves, so new leaders are developed for the benefit of new groups. I've followed this model for nearly thirty years as an apprentice, co-leader, and then leader. It's a natural progression to be recruited, lead with a mentor, and then assume the role of leader. It works, and the proof is in any group that replicates itself. It's biblical, it's honoring, and it's healthy!

Teaching people how to prepare for end-of-life has brought me tremendous satisfaction. I hope you will keep researching, refine your plan, and then share it with trusted family members and friends. I invite you to share the insights from your research with me so I can learn from you. Connect with me online or send me an email at: pastorrickcraig@whenitstime.org.

DISCLAIMER

As you read this manuscript, at no time should you take these suggestions as absolute directives and act upon them as such. While each section is filled with valuable information that you can apply to multiple situations, it is offered as helpful suggestions only. I encourage you to seek the advice of professionals in each field since your situation may differ from mine and others with whom I have worked. Your state laws may be different from mine in California, and your circumstances will certainly not mirror mine or those I have worked with in every scenario. Please take this information as examples only, not legal advice to help you address your specific needs.

Likewise, as a group leader, please recommend to your attendees to always consult a professional related to the areas discussed, obtaining information that is applicable to their own state laws and personal dynamics. To enhance your group meetings, consider inviting professionals from the vocations referenced in the book to offer insight and answer pertinent questions for everyone's benefit.

I have no legal, financial, or marketing relationship with any of the resources listed or references made in this book. The resources listed are solely for your reference and education. There is a plethora of websites available to the reader, and I encourage you to do your own research.

PART ONE

ESTABLISHING YOUR WHEN IT'S TIME® GROUP

OUR GOAL AND STRATEGY

Our goal is to equip as many people as possible to prepare for end-of-life by reading the book series, joining a group, or independently completing their plan for the benefit of their survivors. We want people to read our material, discuss their findings with family members (if appropriate), develop a plan after careful research and mentoring from relevant professionals, share their plan, and then review the plan after a life event (a change that has occurred that does or could affect the plan).

Our strategy to accomplish this goal is to replicate our efforts by training new leaders to teach and assist in pre-planning and survivors' next steps using the book series, seminars, and small groups. Through these seminars and a digital presence, we want to identify and invite potential and established leaders to lead a study using the *When It's Time®* series and their own firsthand experiences to help others go beyond procrastination or apathy to a well-thought-out end-of-life plan. Leader development and replication is the backbone of our goal of equipping thousands of people. This is an intentional approach; make a plan and live out that plan! I applaud you for becoming a group leader and thank you for joining us in this mission.

BECOMING A LEADER

Facilitating a study requires the leader to be prepared. The *When It's Time® Leader's Guide* will assist you whether this is your first time facilitating or you're a seasoned veteran.

There are two approaches you can take as a leader. The first is to complete the material before presenting it to your group. This gives you the advantage of firsthand experience so others can learn from your research and application of knowledge. The second approach is to lead your group as a participant yourself, learning through the discussion, research, and application along with other attendees. Personally, I feel the first approach will make you a more effective leader, and I recommend that you read the book and complete the workbook *before* your group begins. But you need to decide what works best for you.

Next, identify a qualified co-leader to help strategize who to invite to your newly formed group. As the group develops, the leader and co-leader identify an apprentice they can train to be a co-leader and eventually a leader of a group. Leaders produce leaders, and missing this opportunity is depriving someone of the chance and privilege to help others. Group leaders should know from the beginning that their role is to equip new leaders while leading their group.

This leader's guide will walk through each chapter of the *When It's Time®* book by highlighting four segments for the facilitator:

- Goal of the chapter
- Main points of the chapter
- Discussion points
- Group assignments for the chapter

This will provide structure for the group, encouraging the attendees to initiate their own research and share their findings. Within the discussion points section, you will find three types of promptings:

- Notes to Leader
- Points of Interest
- Questions & Answers

Each prompting assists the leader in initiating a topic for discussion, continuing the conversation, or leading group members to an additional topic for discussion. As you become familiar with using the leader's guide, you will develop a rhythm that works well for you.

GROUP DYNAMICS

A *When It's Time®* group meets on a regular basis with the expressed purpose of developing an end-of-life plan, which includes a survivors' next-steps plan.

Group Size

Group size can range from three or four people to twenty or more. Too small and the sharing/learning can be diminished because there is less input. Too large and the amount of information shared can slow the group to a pace where you lose group members. A group size of eight to twelve tends to embody two ideal dynamics: quantity and quality of information. With this group size, the information shared tends to be more relevant, factual, and experiential, while topics are still open for discussion.

Building Trust

If your group has already been meeting, then you know the group's relational dynamics and trust has already developed. If your group is new and attendees are not familiar with one another, start your first meeting with a statement that lays out expectations and boundaries of group participation, and help members get to know each other with an icebreaker question. End-of-life conversations include difficult subjects to talk about, requiring vulnerability. Helping participants get to know each other on a personal level builds the trust needed for tough topics. Managing the personalities in your group to prevent conversation dominators will help create a safe space for the quieter to speak up. Personal history shared voluntarily creates a bond that every group needs. And as a leader, you want this bond to occur sooner rather than later to enhance your group relationships. Group dynamics occur naturally, but when led by a true leader, there's a bonding that can last for months, years, or decades. This bonding is where encouragement is fostered, help shared, and a communal sense of accomplishment is celebrated. Leaders promote this and celebrate it!

Communication

Creating a healthy group requires communication. Consider assigning roles to people—such as someone to manage refreshments for *hospitality*, someone to help celebrate *events* like birthdays and anniversaries, and someone to handle the *calendar* by sending out reminders and announcements. Good communication engages group members and assists in developing community. People can feel disconnected without a reasonable flow of communication. If you want your members to feel included, then communicate with them!

Personalizing Your Teaching

Over the course of time, you may recognize that your delivery method/style changes with the attendees' dynamics, such as a young married group versus a group that is middle-aged or elderly. Because their life stages are different, your content selection and delivery of material will change to fit the group. As the leader, you have the freedom to select or skip content in this guide as you see fit. It takes time and practice, but personalization will enhance your ability to reach any group you are teaching. With each chapter, consider each participant's life experiences and the emotions attached as a result. Your group members will respond differently to each scenario based on their experiences, so lead with curiosity and grace, and others will follow. I was recently reminded of a saying that is true: "Others may have a different opinion of you than you have of yourself." It's a good reminder that we should be mindful of other people's experience and default to saying, "tell me more about that to help me understand." When we remove pride and become a student, we learn to be better leaders.

Duration & Reflection

Since certain chapters could require making appointments with professionals to develop a plan, purchase a policy, sign contracts, etc., your group should consider meeting for sixteen weeks or more if you are accustomed to meeting weekly, such as a church group. This is common for groups to meet for this length of time. Conversely, there could be *When It's Time®* groups that meet for several weeks, then decide to finish on their own and report back at a predetermined date. I discourage this because you lose the natural bonding that every group needs to thrive. During your last two to three group meetings, have an honest and open discussion about the group's future. Ask for feedback on what to study next and invite opinions. Don't be surprised if half of your group feels they have met their goal while the other half wish to continue. Both are right. Accept it. Sometimes a break may be needed before your next study. These decisions are the result of effective communication and based on your group's dynamics. The last type of group could be a three- or four-part seminar for a community group (an organization reaching out to their community as an example); then you should consider condensing the material by touching on a few key points from each chapter while leaving extra time for question and discussions.

All group leaders want to know how they performed as a facilitator, whether they admit it or not. Group leaders who want to continually improve their skills will initiate a time of reflection by members. This reflection can be verbal or written. Personally, I have promoted both because some people can be very vocal while others, who are more reserved, prefer a written survey. Both are fine, and both are beneficial, so do what is best for you based on knowing your members and group dynamics. You can download a Reflection Survey at www.WhenItsTime.org.

PREPARING FOR YOUR FIRST MEETING

Before the Meeting Begins

Send an email or text two to three days before your meeting as a reminder of the start time, location, and the chapter you will be studying. Include in your communication that group members should read the material before your meeting to be prepared for a conversation and questions about the material. Prepare refreshments and gather name tag supplies if you are a new group or have new members joining an existing group.

Welcome 15-20 Min

After establishing a start time for your group, there will be people arriving early, on time, and a few that will come in late. Leave a cushion for this by having a light refreshment available so people can greet one another and share stories individually through general conversation, in preparation for the group to begin.

Recap 15 Min

A leader should take fifteen minutes to recap the last meeting as a reminder and to ask if members have completed their homework/ goals. Seldom will you have 100 percent say yes. This is a suitable time to ask, why not? Expect answers to range from "I was too busy," and "I'm waiting for an appointment from professional to ask questions," to "emotionally it was too difficult," and other assorted reasons. This is normal and it's all right. Encourage them to continue but keep notes because you may be going too fast as a group, or you could have a small contingency that are not ready to complete their work. Don't let this contingency stall your group, but rather, have a separate conversation with them, giving them permission to take their time, so they do not hold the group back.

Facilitation 45-60 Min

As a facilitator, your role is to present the material topically while asking members to respond with their own experiences and what they have learned from the book series. Encourage discussion and input during your meeting. Accept silence when it happens, allowing people to comprehend comments and formulate thoughts. You will have mixed responses, so give people time to process their feelings and articulate their answers. Mentor your co-leader and apprentice, allowing them to lead part of your study.

Wrap-Up 10 Min

Before the group closes for the day/night, ask for feedback about the quantity of material you covered. Is it too much, too little, or exactly right? Does the group need to slow down or is the pace acceptable? As a leader, asking for input and making adjustments will promote group interest and longevity. Then, encourage them to apply what they have read and work through their workbook. Keep in mind that the workbook will be your gauge in quantifying the progress, interest level of the material, and targeted finish date. Outline the focus and homework for the next meeting. End your meeting (on time!) with encouragement and offer to talk with or meet anyone who needs special attention. Follow up with members with a phone call later in the week if you sense they are struggling.

PART TWO

BUILDING YOUR END-OF-LIFE PLAN

CHAPTER ONE

INVESTIGATING LIFE INSURANCE

GOAL OF THE CHAPTER

Life insurance is important to cover your family financially. In this chapter, you'll learn the process for purchasing a policy, what type of policy you need, and how much coverage based on your family dynamics.

MAIN POINTS

- Buying life insurance is always a good idea. It can provide for your heirs or cover other costs later on. Reasons you might purchase life insurance include:
  - » To pay off debt.
  - » To replace primary income for survivors.
  - » To cover expenses for a child with special needs.
  - » To pay for final expenses.
  - » To protect parents and grandparents financially should a younger family member die, and as a result, the survivors turn to older family members for ongoing financial support.
  - » To cover the cost of the spouse's contribution.

  - » To pay for children's expenses.
  - » To buy out a business partner.
- Everyone has different needs when it comes to life insurance. The type and amount of insurance you need will depend on your life dynamics.
- The two main types of life insurance are whole life insurance (a policy which stays in force) and term life insurance (a policy with an expiration date).

DISCUSSION POINTS

Using Agents or Brokers

Point of interest: There are online companies (acting as brokers representing a host of life insurance companies) selling life insurance at competitive prices compared to brick-and-mortar companies, which typically have higher-priced policies.

Question: Should you use an agent or a broker? What is the advantage of one over the other?

Answer: An agent working for one company in the brick-and-mortar business is there to represent you throughout the process. They are your advocates. An online company can offer similar services but will often have different representatives with each call, meaning less *personal attention.*

Whole vs. Term Policies

Question: Can anyone tell me the difference between whole and term life insurance?

Answer: Think of "whole" as coverage for your whole life versus "term" being for a designated period of time, such as ten to twenty years.

Question: Which is best for you?

Note to leader: Encourage a discussion.

Answer: Not having coverage for your family could necessitate having to sell a family home or other assets for needed cash. It could mean eliminating future plans for your family or being unable to help with the ongoing financial support of family members with needs. This is one reason a person should consider coverage for their "whole life" or for a "term" due to life dynamics.

Stacking Policies

Point of interest: It's becoming more common to purchase multiple term life insurance policies for prolonged coverage, such as purchasing a twenty-year policy, then ten years into that policy, purchasing an additional ten- or twenty-year policy.

Question: Why should you consider stacking policies to prolong your term coverage? How would this benefit you?

Answer: Purchasing a policy at a younger age, then stacking another policy years later, prolongs your coverage while taking advantage of smaller premiums.

Policies for Newborns

Question: Why should you consider a whole life policies for a newborn (15 days or older)?

Answer: A grandparent who purchases a policy for a grandchild with the intent to pay the premium for a limited time and then turn it over to the parent can help provide for the child in the future and motivate the parents to protect their family. Additionally, when purchasing a policy for a newborn, the policy premium is extremely low, and a whole life policy can accrue a substantial principle with regular deposits, which could fund your child or grandchild's college or first home purchase. This takes planning and investing, but it can offer many benefits.

Amount of Coverage Needed

Note to leader: Family dynamics vary, but there are commonalities when understanding the need for life insurance. Follow the template on pages 24–25 of the workbook to determine the true dollar-value coverage your family needs instead of guessing at an amount.

Question: If you currently have life insurance, have you reviewed your policy to see if you are under-insured, right where you should be, or over-insured?

Ask for a policy review with your agent to help determine the right coverage, then make adjustments.

Protecting Your Assets if a Family Member Dies

Point of interest: It is common when an adult son or daughter passes away to have the surviving spouse ask their parents to help financially with everyday costs if they did not have an active life insurance policy. This could result in hundreds of thousands of dollars of support from the parents' savings over time.

Note to leader: There is an alternative to the scenario above, although it could be an emotional conversation to have with your group and for your group members to have with their adult children. Propose to parents with married children that they purchase a life insurance policy for each married adult child (if they do not currently have a life insurance policy), with the understanding that the parent will pay the premiums for one year until their children can build the premium into their budget. Then, they turn the premium payments over to their son/daughter. Why is this important? To protect their assets from requests for financial support that could go on for years or decades.

Question: If you have a son/daughter that is married, with or without children, do they and their spouse have a well-thought-out life insurance policy that will provide financial support for the survivor over the next 10 to 20 years?

As a leader, using the scenario above, explain problems and solutions, then open it up for discussion. If you have group members that have experienced this scenario, let them share in detail as a good teaching moment.

Beneficiaries

Point of interest: There are options on how to designate beneficiaries for your life insurance policy. You can name a Trust as the beneficiary (there could be tax liabilities) or you can list beneficiaries directly by name.

Question: Have you considered what method of naming beneficiaries will work best for your beneficiaries?

Meet with your tax preparer to have a conversation about helping your beneficiaries to avoid paying taxes on the distribution.

Question: If you have a life insurance policy, do you know. . .

- Where it is kept?
- If the agent is still in business?
- If the policy is still active?
- If the policy has been reviewed for changes to beneficiaries?

ASSIGNMENTS

Using the workbook calculation template on pages 24–25, determine a dollar amount you believe fits your life dynamics. If you have an active term or whole life policy, review the dollar value and determine if it still fits your needs.

Determine if your spending plan (budget) will allow for a new policy. Keep in mind that you may have to make changes in your spending plan or develop a new spending plan to achieve the goal of purchasing a life insurance policy.

Decide who in your family will be covered (e.g., husband, wife, infant after the 15-day waiting period, etc.).

If you have an active policy, review the beneficiaries to determine whether this is still accurate.

If you need a new policy or want to stack a policy in addition to your active policy, research online about companies and their premiums and learn the terminology and sales points they use.

Make appointments with two to three agents for a discussion about their recommended dollar coverage, who should be covered and why, term versus a whole life policy, and premium amount.

CHAPTER TWO

DEVELOPING YOUR ESTATE PLAN

GOAL OF THE CHAPTER

Learn how estate planning can protect your assets. We'll explore distribution of your assets and guardianship of your minor children to make sure your wishes are protected and fulfilled.

MAIN POINTS

- Estate planning, when completed, has numerous benefits. A Will or Trust allows your wishes to be conducted without interruption and avoids a prolonged probate process, serving your survivors at their time of need.
- A Will or Trust must withstand the scrutiny of the court, therefore, downloading a generic document online should be done with great caution.
- Choosing the right type of Trust can provide for your survivors, meeting their specific needs.
- A simple Will protects your minor children with declared guardianship if both parents were to die.

- A well-thought-out plan can mitigate family arguments.
- When choosing a Trustee or Executor, understand their particular roles and take into consideration their qualifications.

DISCUSSION POINTS

Wills & Trusts

Question: If you have a Will or Trust, do you know where it is, and do you know if the attorney who drafted it is still in practice? Have you reviewed it within the last two to three years or after a recent "life event" (a change within your Trust that could cause you to consider making a change to a beneficiary, Trustee, or Executor)?

Note to leader: Once your attorney completes your Trust, you must move your assets into the Trust to take full advantage of the law. If your assets (real estate, bank accounts, tangible assets, for example) are not titled in your Trust's name, then they are outside of the Trust and susceptible to probate.

Question: If you have a Trust, have you moved your assets into the Trust so they are protected?

Note: Ask your group to explain what that process was like. Were they given a document by their attorney containing what assets needed to be moved into the Trust?

Question: If you have children who are minors, do you have a Will or Trust designating who the guardians will be should both parents die?

Without this, minors can be assigned to the court before their future is determined, which could last for months or years.

Types of Trusts

Point of interest: There are several types of Trusts to address different family dynamics, such as situations where you need support for family members with special needs, asset protection, long-term succession, income provision, prevention of direct access to funds by heirs, and more. Choosing what is best for you should involve an estate attorney's mentoring.

Question: Who in our group has met with an attorney to discuss particular types of Trusts? What was the result of that discussion?

Your Estate Team

Point of interest: Choosing a Trustee or Executor requires personal qualifications to meet the needs of each role. Consider each qualification.

Note to leader: It is common that people do not understand the difference between a Trustee and Executor. Take time to discuss this for clarity.

Trustee

- Trustees have a fiduciary duty to manage the Trust with care, loyalty, and prudence.
- Responsibilities can include investing Trust assets, distributing income, keeping accurate records, and filing tax returns for the Trust.
- Trustees can have ongoing responsibilities, lasting years or generations until the Trust is financially exhausted.
- Trustees can be family members or trusted advisers, or corporate entities like banks or Trust companies.

Executor

- Executors are responsible for managing the estate of the decedent during the probate process.
- Executors will inventory assets, pay debts and taxes, and distribute the remaining assets according to the Will or Trust.

- Executors are fiduciaries, which carries a legal responsibility.
- The Executor's role is typically finished once asset distribution is completed, which may take months or years.

Question: Has anyone met with a Fiduciary Adviser to learn more about their role and the fees? Did you read about Fiduciary Advisers in the workbook? What did you learn?

Point of interest: There are times when a Fiduciary Adviser is the best person to manage your Trust. Pre-planners can avoid family disputes by not designating a family member who is not capable or qualified to manage your estate, but rather, by a Fiduciary Adviser who is licensed and proven to be competent.

Question: Have you named a Durable Power of Attorney (DPOA) for your finances and a Durable Power of Attorney for your healthcare needs? One person can fulfill both roles, or two separate people can be named.

ASSIGNMENTS

If you currently have a Will or Trust, locate it and determine the last time it was reviewed. If your document has not been reviewed and updated based on changes you would like to make or within three to five years, make an appointment with your attorney to update it. Changes cannot be made after your death. Laws change, so your old Trust may not serve your survivors well, based on new laws.

Parents with minor children, at minimum, need a Will to determine their children's guardianship if both parents were to die. Meet with an attorney to have a simple Will drafted for their protection.

If you do not have a current Will or Trust, research online about the types of Trusts that may fit your need. Next, call estate attorneys and inquire about their fees to develop a Trust that is designed to meet your family dynamics. After researching the attorney's business history, ratings, and costs, make an appointment to begin the process.

Consider who you would name as Trustee of your Trust, your Financial DPOA, and your Healthcare DPOA, then approach these people and seek their approval. Finally, name them in your Trust documents as they are developed or updated.

CHAPTER THREE

GIVING THE GIFT OF ORGAN DONATION

GOAL OF THE CHAPTER

The process of eye, organ, and tissue donation remains a mystery for too many people. In this chapter, we'll answer the questions that prevent people from signing up to be a donor and encourage them to take the next steps.

MAIN POINTS

- There is a need for organ, eye, or tissue donation to save or prolong lives.
- It's simple to sign up at donatelife.net or at your local Department of Motor Vehicles, with the ability to opt out at any time.
- Many religious tenets/traditions approve of being a donor.
- There are no associated costs with being a donor.
- Myths and misperceptions about donation can prevent someone from signing up. Dispelling these inaccuracies with accurate information will help you make a decision.

DISCUSSION POINTS

Signing Up to be a Donor

Question: Who in our group is signed up to be an organ, eye, or tissue donor? What led you to decide this?

Donation Recovery

Note to leader: The questions below are to help show the lack of knowledge concerning being a donor and will reveal myths people share prohibiting them from signing up. Each question is answered in When It's Time® pages 46–48.

Question: Does anyone know someone who had signed up as a donor, and upon their death, an organ, eye, or tissue recovery was performed?

Note to leader: Use these follow-up questions to draw out these topics:

- Are you aware of the steps taken for the recovery of the organ, eye, or tissue?
- What was the final outcome concerning the time it took from the point of death until their body was delivered to the funeral home/mortuary?
- After an organ recovery, was an open casket viewing an option?

- Were there costs involved for the surviving family?

Point of interest: An open casket viewing is possible even in the case of organ, eye, or tissue recovery.

Religious Views

Question: If you are a person of faith, what does your religion or denomination have to say about organ, eye, or tissue donation?

Note to leader: Review the faith tenets/traditions listed in When It's Time® pages 48–53 as needed.

Costs of Donation

Question: Do you think there are costs associated with organ, eye, or tissue donation?

Answer: No.
Chapter eight discusses interviewing funeral directors for pre-planning, so keep this question about any costs as a donor in mind for that conversation. Your funeral director will reassure you that there are no costs associated with donation.

ASSIGNMENTS

After reading the chapter on organ, eye, and tissue donation, pursue finding answers to your questions that have made you reluctant to become a donor. If needed, peruse the donatelife.net website for additional information.

If you are a person of faith and need additional information or reassurance from your house of worship, make an appointment with your pastor or spiritual leader for clarity and affirmation.

If you feel ready, register as an organ, eye, or tissue donor at donatelife.net or through your local DMV.

Chapter 4

RECEIVING HOSPICE CARE

GOAL OF THE CHAPTER

Myths, stigmas, and a lack of understanding about hospice benefits preclude people from seeking care. We'll address each issue with facts, enabling a hospice candidate to make sound decisions to benefit both them and their family members or caregivers.

MAIN POINTS

- Learning the hospice qualification process, interviewing providers, and finally receiving care takes time and guidance to avoid mistakes.
- Qualification for hospice begins with your doctor.
- There is a difference between palliative and hospice care. You could qualify for palliative care long before hospice care.
- Hospice accreditation organizations have established guidelines and standards.
- Learning how to interview hospice providers within your area will help you make an informed choice.

- Dispelling myths about hospice care will help you make the right decision for you.
- Understanding the distinction of certification periods is critical—two ninety-day periods or an unlimited number of sixty-day periods.
- Having a comprehensive discussion about hospice care and the training offered to a family member or caregiver brings hope and confidence.

DISCUSSION POINTS

Obstacles to Hospice Care

You may not be a candidate today or anytime soon for hospice care, but if you were, are there any reasons you would *not* pursue this benefit?

Note to leader: Present this as a discussion.

Taken from multiple discussions with hospice representatives and research, here are the top five reasons why people do not pursue hospice care.

Reason #1: I don't know how to qualify.

Response: Hospice care begins with your doctor, who approves you as a client.

Reason #2: My family member had hospice, and they had problems with their provider. I wouldn't want the same problems.

Response: There are ten key questions to ask your hospice provider during your interview. Not asking these questions could result in a lack of understanding, and therefore, unmet expectations. Asking the right questions usually results in receiving the anticipated care. Pages 59–61 in *When It's Time*® outline these questions.

Reason #3: My family members would not know how to care for me, so I'll put it off for as long as possible.

Response: Part of hospice care is training your family members or caregivers to care for you. This enhances your care and gives them access to your hospice nurse.

Reason #4: If I sign up for hospice care, then I've just admitted that I only have days or weeks to live.

Response: Signing up for hospice results in improved home care, and your life expectancy is well over two months, based on the average client's benefit period.

Reason #5: I don't like the idea that once I sign up for hospice, I have to sign a Do Not Resuscitate (DNR), which means they will let me die earlier versus living longer.

Response: A DNR is not required. The goal of hospice care is to let you define your end-of-life and how that will play out.

Certification Periods

Note to leader: Present this as a point that needs to be discussed with their hospice representative.

Certification periods define the length and frequency the hospice benefit is available. The hospice candidate can choose two ninety-day periods or an unlimited number of sixty-day periods. Choosing the wrong certification period can result in the client paying out-of-pocket. I highly advise you to have this discussion with the hospice representative to make the proper decision that is best for you.

ASSIGNMENTS

If you have a family member or friend (survivor) who took this journey with a loved one through the process of qualifying/receiving palliative or hospice care, talk to them about the process.

- Did their loved one postpone care and why?
- What questions did they ask the hospice provider candidate during the interview process?
- How long was their loved one receiving hospice care?
- What benefit period did they sign up for? Two ninety-day periods or unlimited sixty-day periods, and why?

- What advice can they provide to help you in decision-making?

Research the hospice providers in your area so you have a selection ready when you qualify. Check their accreditation, read reviews, and explore what services they provide. Hospice providers include a host of professionals as part of your care, such as clergy, counselors, home health aides, hospice physicians, nurses, social workers, trained volunteers, and speech/physical/occupational therapists. In your research for an accredited provider, be confident that these services or similar services are guaranteed before making a decision.

CHAPTER FIVE

STRUGGLING WITH SUDDEN DEATH

GOAL OF THE CHAPTER

A sudden death can be devastating, leaving the deceased's loved ones debilitated with grief, which makes performing basic tasks difficult. This chapter will help you cope with unexpected circumstances by outlining helpful steps you can take before a death occurs so that you have a plan in place already.

MAIN POINTS

Understanding the series of events that take place in a sudden death situation will help you develop a plan. Being organized prior to death will allow your team to assist you from the very beginning. Your plan should include, but is not limited to:

- Having a basic understanding of how first responders operate if called to your home.
- Having a list of medications and medical conditions for each person at your home will help you answer detailed questions from first responders.

- Making available documents such as a DNR upon request for first responders.
- Having all documentation prepared in advance that would be required by your state, funeral director, and officiant for a funeral or memorial.
- Using the Survivor Checklist© as a guide for you and your team when death occurs.

DISCUSSION POINTS

Information to Gather

Question: If an accident or death were to occur at your residence, do you have the appropriate numbers recorded on your phone or on paper for easy access and immediate contact?

Answer: **911** should be your immediate number to reach out for help. List key family members or friends who live close enough to assist you.

Question: If first responders are called, what information do you think you should have available within easy reach?

- A list of medications the person is prescribed.
- Any evidence that the person is under the influence of illegal drugs or medication not prescribed.
- Any medical conditions first responders should know about (e.g., durable medical equipment, pacemaker, diabetic, heart issues, mental illness, etc.)

DNRs and Death Certificates

> Question: Why might a Coroner Investigator be involved in a sudden death?

Answer: *Cause* and *manner* of death are two qualifiers for why a Coroner Investigator would be involved. Cause is the medical reason for death. Manner is how the person died. Knowing this before an end-of-life event will assist survivors in understanding and accepting the process.

> Question: Do you or your loved one have a DNR? Why or why not?

Personal Experiences

> Question: Can anyone share an experience with sudden death and the events that followed for the benefit of our group members?

Question: Can anyone share their experience with confusion after the death of a loved one that might benefit our group?

Developing a Plan

Note to leader: Open up dialogue with these questions.

Question: With the understanding of events that take place after an anticipated or sudden death, does this motivate you to start pre-planning or have your plan available at a moment's notice? If not, why not? What challenges do you see with developing a plan?

ASSIGNMENTS

If you have not already, begin assembling documentation needed as if you had placed a call to **911** for help. This documentation is what responders will ask for immediately upon entering your house or public space. Here's a tip: If appropriate, have these on your phone as documents that you can pull up if you are away from home.

File important medical documents like directives or DNRs in a location that is accessible should you need to take your loved one to the hospital (or they, you). Make sure your family members know where to find these forms. (Medical facilities will not keep documents such as DNRs on file unless the person has been a prior patient.)

Put together your team using the Survivor Checklist©. Make sure they understand their roles before a sudden death occurs. It will take one phone call or email to each for them to begin assisting you. The Survivor Checklist© will be one of your most used and appreciated documents after a death.

CHAPTER SIX

COPING WITH MISCARRIAGE, STILLBIRTH, AND INFANT LOSS

GOAL OF THE CHAPTER

Miscarriage, stillbirth, and infant loss happen too often to ignore the physical or emotional impact it has on parents, especially the mother. In this chapter, we'll discuss how planning for the worst, while hoping for the best, can help parents prepare for what to expect.

MAIN POINTS

- Having a "what-if" conversation before or during pregnancy, uncomfortable as it might be, will help prepare expectant parents concerning the questions and processes they will face in the event of a loss.
- Your Company Bereavement Policy (CBP) may provide extended time off for recovery, or it may not consider pregnancy loss a qualifying event.
- It is common for cemeteries to have a section

of plots and a columbarium (with niches) reserved for interment for babies free-of-charge.

- Giving your baby a name gives them an identity and may help with your emotional recovery.
- Legal definitions and personal convictions will guide parents in determining the legal disposition of their baby because the death of a pre-born is treated differently than a minor or adult death.
- Parents who have experienced a loss need support. Sharing your knowledge, compassion, and grace can make a difference.

DISCUSSION POINTS

Note to leader: Your group may have members who are still in their childbearing years, and you may have group members who are parents watching their children/grandchildren plan or become pregnant. Of all the chapters, this may be the most difficult for group members who have experienced infant loss. Proceed with sensitivity and grace in your questions. With this in mind, I suggest saying: "If anyone would prefer not to engage in this conversation, that is all right because we don't want you to experience unnecessary discomfort. Although, if you choose to engage, we can learn from you, and you may find more healing from sharing your experience. Regardless of your choice, we respect you and support you."

"What-If" Conversations

Question: If you are a parent or plan to be, have you ever had a conversation about the "what-ifs" with your partner? What did this conversation cover, and how did you feel after the conversation(s)? Was there a plan or collective understanding on how to respond if a miscarriage or stillbirth occurred?

Note to leader: Explain that the following guideline for the "what-if" conversation between a couple can promote an environment for a healthy conversation.

Timing: An abrupt, impromptu conversation is not recommended for this challenging topic, but rather, plan an uninterrupted time.

Grace: Each person has the right to be heard and not interrupted because their feelings and input have value.

Love: A one-time conversation may not yield all the answers you hoped for, so circle back as needed.

Hope: If you are a person of faith, prayer before, during, and after seeking guidance provides hope.

Question: If you attended any childbirth preparation classes, did they talk about pregnancy loss? If so, what did they say? If this was a topic discussed, what did you learn from the instruction?

WHEN A LOSS HAPPENS

Note to leader: Open this segment as discussion points and thoughts.

With an infant loss, your medical staff will ask a multitude of questions, such as:

- Do you want to take pictures with your baby? The medical provider will tell you that it's normal and they will take the pictures in most cases. How do you think you would respond to this offer and why?
- Do you want to spend time alone with your baby? Spending time with your baby is suggested to help you process what has happened, and it's your only and last chance for this opportunity. If offered, do you think you would take advantage of this time to be alone?
- Would you like to name your baby? Laws vary from state to state, but depending upon the gestation period, a death certificate can be required, for which choosing a name in advance would be helpful.

Disposition Decisions

Note to leader: Open this discussion point as "here are some of the facts," and then open it up for discussion.

As parents, you will be asked about the disposition of your baby after a miscarriage or stillbirth.

You have options. You can choose burial with a casket or cremation at a local cemetery. Cemeteries often offer a plot or niche at no charge as a way of honoring your baby and you. But you are still required to fund the casket or urn and other elements of a service. Investigating these options in advance will provide information for decision-making while your cognitive skill level is still high, rather than making decisions in the delivery room. If this research is too difficult for you, consider having a trusted family member or friend do the research for you, and if needed, call upon them for assistance.

Grief Support

Question: Do you know if your Company Bereavement Policy will serve you well at the time of need?

Note to leader: Your CBP may not consider a miscarriage or stillbirth as a family death that qualifies for bereavement leave, but rather, an illness—requiring you to take sick leave or paid time off.

Question: Are you aware of grief support resources in your community? Have you or would you take advantage of them? What would be most helpful to you after a loss, and when might you feel ready to go through this process?

Point of interest: There are counties that offer up to one year of counseling for the parents of a miscarried or stillborn baby.

Question: Does your county offer this benefit at no charge? Will you take advantage of this offer to help recover? Do you know of anyone who has received counseling after an infant loss? If so, have a conversation with them about their experience.

It's possible that they will say, "I didn't get much out of it because it was too early." Conversely, parents who postpone counseling and attended later will say, "I'm glad I waited because I wasn't ready for counseling after I lost my baby."

ASSIGNMENTS

Read this chapter in *When It's Time*® and complete the corresponding workbook chapter. Use that as a launch pad for a conversation about the "what ifs."

If you are planning or expecting a child, or if you have experienced a miscarriage or stillbirth and did not name your baby, consider doing it now to provide an identity for your baby. This could be part of your short-term or long-term recovery.

Examine your CBP to determine whether infant loss qualifies for bereavement leave.

If you need counseling for infant loss, whether it was recent or years ago, find a counselor or therapist because the pain can continue for a prolonged period of time. You are not required to harbor this pain; instead, learn how to release it or live with it. If you know anyone who has received counseling after an infant loss, have a conversation with them about their experience. Then, explore what counseling resources and benefits might be available to you.

CHAPTER SEVEN

CLARIFYING BEREAVEMENT LEAVE

GOAL OF THE CHAPTER

This chapter equips an employee to negotiate for paid time off (PTO) and develop a plan with management to return to the workplace. We'll also cover how employees can welcome back a coworker after bereavement leave.

MAIN POINTS

- A Human Resource Department Director can help you understand your CBP and how to negotiate for additional PTO. If there is an imminent death within your family, consider approaching your employer in advance.
- Meeting with your immediate supervisor to make a plan before your return will ease your transition back to work.
- Part of your reintroduction plan may include using the "Returning Employee Letter" to reduce awkwardness and stress.
- There are comments that should *not* be made by management and coworkers to the return-

ing employee. This chapter offers alternatives that *are* respectful, encouraging, and honoring.

DISCUSSION POINTS

Note to leader: It is important to communicate that only one state—Oregon—has a bereavement law, and the federal government has no such law. When your group members realize there is no law to protect them, it highlights the need to understand their CBP and how to negotiate for PTO.

Understanding Your Company Bereavement Policy

Question: Have you examined your CBP for bereavement leave? If so, what are the number of days an employee can use strictly for bereavement? Is there language suggesting you can use additional PTO or have fellow employees donate time to you? Does it explain the process on how to solicit donated PTO from fellow employees?

Returning to Work

Question: How would you use the "Returning Employee Letter" at your workplace when you consider the work culture within your company? How do you think working with your management would enhance the workplace culture?

Question: Who within our group has used their bereavement leave? Would you walk us through the process you took from the time of your loved one's passing to your return to work? Were you met with compassion and grace, or did your workplace seem annoyed or inconvenienced because you were off? What went well, and what do you wish had been different?

Question: Review the responses to returning employees (pp. 103–106 in *When It's Time*®), both helpful and hurtful, in this chapter. Did you experience any of these comments? If you haven't taken a bereavement leave from work before, which of these comments would resonate with you if you did?

Managing Bereaved Employees

Question: If you are in management within your company, have you had any experience welcoming a subordinate back into the workplace? What did you do intentionally to welcome the employee back to work? Or what happened if you did not have a plan (positive and negative outcomes)?

If you are currently operating in management within your organization, consider that this chapter can change company culture to be more sensitive without adding a financial burden. Two intentional ways are:

- By simply offering compassion and undivided attention by listening to the employee and by working on a plan for reintroduction.
- Allowing colleagues to donate time to other employees as an act of love and mercy. Every HR Director wants to reduce PTO on the books because it is a financial liability. By reducing this line item, whether through gifted PTO, resignation, retirement, or termination, the organization accomplishes financial liability reduction while enhancing the work culture.

ASSIGNMENTS

Review your Employee Handbook (EH) for your CBP benefit, if you have a CBP at all. Most organizations have a CBP of three days. Then review your EH to see if bereavement leave also includes colleagues donating their PTO to you and the process involved.

If your family currently has a family member with declining health and death is imminent, review the

"Returning Employee Letter" and rewrite it to fit your scenario so it's ready to go when the situation arises.

If you have a management role in your company, consider putting this topic on your agenda for discussion, review, and changes to your policy.

If you have a colleague currently using the bereavement leave benefit, how will you respond to them upon their return? If you are in management within your company, how will you lead your team upon the bereaved employee's return?

As a person who can mentor family and friends, is there someone you know who could use help with their return to work or re-engaging with life in general due to the loss of a loved one? What will you do?

CHAPTER EIGHT

CHOOSING THE RIGHT FUNERAL HOME

GOAL OF THE CHAPTER

After completing this chapter, pre-planners or survivors will have the capacity to answer questions and make good decisions about choosing the right funeral home/director and negotiating costs to fit their needs and finances. Additionally, they'll have a working understanding of the administrative needs involved with death, funeral home administrative requests, and survivor responsibilities.

MAIN POINTS

- Choosing a funeral home/director takes time and research and tours of facilities to become familiar with this industry.
- Funeral/memorial costs vary with each funeral home/mortuary; each will offer package deals to attract business.
- What is the difference between a funeral home and mortuary?
- Your choice of disposition will depend on

your finances, personal wishes, and theological tenets (if you're a person of faith).

- Death certificate data is required from family members, Trustees, Executors, or those with Durable Power of Attorney. Collection of this data is much easier while pre-planning.
- Obituaries are traditionally written after a person's death. However, I encourage the pre-planner to use the workbook templates in advance.

DISCUSSION POINTS

Finding a Funeral Home/Mortuary

Note to leader: The following question has the potential to have little to no response, or it can open up a conversation that becomes very emotional. Begin by reviewing the funeral home questionnaire (p. 112 of the book and p. 78 of the workbook) as a group. These points are helpful to prepare for your appointment and to reflect upon afterward as you determine which funeral home/mortuary will best fit your needs.

> Question: Who in our group has started the section on "pre-planning" by visiting a funeral home or mortuary? What steps did you take before you visited your first funeral home or mortuary? Describe your experience.

Question: On the funeral home questionnaire, which points are most important to you and why?

Note to leader: A funeral director will ask if you are pre-need or at-need to determine your sense of urgency and how to greet you as a client. While both types of clients will be there to investigate costs and services provided, the grieving survivor may require more time and repetition to absorb the information. Having a family member or friend present to take notes will help the pre-planner or survivor with recall when decision-making is needed.

Disposition & Death Certificates

Question: What are your personal preferences for disposition, and why did you choose them?

Note to leader: Have one of your group members read the section in chapter eight of When It's Time® about the information needed for a death certificate (pages 120–121).

Question: When we consider that the average number of pieces of information needed to complete a death certificate is seventeen, what documents have you already assembled or can you easily locate?

Gathering the required information and making it available to other family members today will assist your survivors in the future.

Writing an Obituary

Note to leader: Review the obituary formula (pp. 121–122 in the book; p. 85 in the workbook) as a group.

Point of interest: Obituary information usually includes 20 to 25 pieces of information. When used to author an accurate and honoring document, it will flow like a relevant story.

Question: Has anyone in our group written an obituary for a family member or friend—or yourself? What information did you include? Would you like to share what you wrote with the group?

ASSIGNMENTS

Research your local funeral homes and mortuaries and review the services they provide, the costs related to both cremation and burial with a casket, the details of "all-inclusive" deals offered, and the pictures posted online—if available. Online reviews can offer a general consensus on customer satisfaction, but keep them in context—negative reviews might be written by someone at-need, whose expectations were unrealistic or uninformed because of their grief.

When comparing venues, consider where your service will be held to make sure it meets your criteria for costs, aesthetics, theology, timing, and availability.

Talk to family members and friends who have worked with any funeral home/mortuary to glean what they experienced, then ask them, "If you had to do it again, would you do it the same way? If not, what would you change?"

Collect information for a death certificate, because you have the best recall for both family and personal history as a pre-planner. Then begin answering the questions found in the book and workbook. Once completed, share them with your anticipated survivors.

Writing your own obituary, or creating the template for it, is an act of love for your survivors. Follow the templates and begin writing drafts, sharing the finished draft with your family.

CHAPTER NINE

PLANNING A FUNERAL OR MEMORIAL SERVICE

GOAL OF THE CHAPTER

Designing a funeral or memorial service has multiple elements requiring attention to make it flow well and be memorable and honoring. From the officiant's message to pictures and music, this chapter breaks down each element, equipping you to assess costs and create a plan for the details of a service that can be handed off to your survivors or held to honor a loved one.

MAIN POINTS

- Finding the appropriate venue for civilians, law enforcement officers, and veterans is the result of asking the right questions.
- An officiant should be experienced and a great listener to craft a message based on your or the decedent's values and faith.
- Guest speakers are a key component of the service. Having a variety of well-chosen guest speakers can be honoring; but the wrong guest speaker could be dishonoring.

- Family and organizational traditions can enhance your service or be a distraction, so choose wisely.
- Military veterans receive special benefits when it comes to funerals or memorial services. Application for these benefits can be done pre-need or at-need.
- Consider your wishes and your budget when deciding whether and where to hold a reception after the service.
- Leveraging social media or digital communication for a death notification can help you alert family and friends of an upcoming funeral or memorial service.

DISCUSSION POINTS

Note to leader: This set of questions is designed to open up the conversation and promote research for both the pre-need and at-need scenarios.

The Venue

Question: Why is the venue so important when planning a funeral or memorial service?

Note to leader: Review each item below for insight into the particulars of venues.

At a funeral home/mortuary, consider:

A funeral home/mortuary will have a chapel to rent. Why might one choose this venue over another? What do you think the cost is for a service at this venue?

Note: Costs vary greatly from one funeral home/mortuary to another. Pre-planning allows you to compare and choose in advance.

If you have pictures or a video to be shown on the screen, is there a separate cost for this and who will run the equipment?

Answer: Yes, they will operate the equipment, but at a cost.

When the funeral/mortuary staff members are present, there is a cost, called "professional fees." Has anyone used a funeral home/mortuary for a service and what services did they provide as "professional fees?"

A funeral home/mortuary usually has an area for the reception. Will there be a cost associated with this component?

Answer: Yes, and costs vary based on the size of the area and the amenities available. Has anyone used a funeral home/mortuary for a reception? What did they charge and what were the restrictions?

If your reception involves food and drink, this will require a catering firm to supply the food, beverage, and labor. Do you think this is more or less expensive than having the reception at a restaurant or catered at a family member's or friend's home? Is there a greater chance of having guests stay at your funeral home/mortuary of choice for the reception versus driving to another venue for the reception?

Answer: Yes, staying at the same location as the service drastically increases the percentage of people who will remain for the reception.

Note: Comparing costs for having a reception at a local restaurant versus the funeral home will assist you in decision-making.

For a house of worship, consider:

Costs vary when having the service at a house of worship. Some will charge for cleaning, sound/video technicians, and reception area.

A rental fee for the worship center can be a cost item with some houses of worship, while others do not charge.

The ability to have a screen to project pictures and videos depends upon the size of the worship center. Small worship centers can lack this amenity, while large facilities can excel with their equipment and ability to project quality images and sound. How important is this feature to you?

Aesthetics play a significant role in the quality of presentation for a service. If a house of worship is small and unequipped to provide the aesthetics you desire, then consider a different venue. What are your thoughts on this?

Just like a funeral home/mortuary, the amenities offered should meet your expectations when considering parking, cleanliness, bathrooms, audio visual/sound equipment, technicians to operate the equipment, and a reception area.

Receptions at a house of worship could be restricted by the size of the kitchen available for members to cook or a catering company to use (or the lack thereof). In addition, most houses of worship do not allow alcohol, so if this is important to you, consider an alternative venue.

Choosing an Officiant

Choosing an officiant often comes from a recommendation by the funeral home/mortuary/national cemetery when the survivors do not have a relationship with a house of worship leader. As a pre-planner, you have time to find an officiant if you are willing to invest in this element of the service. Where will you begin?

During your interview with each venue, ask for a list of recommended officiants and call them to begin communication. Ask the officiants you interview *how they obtain information about you or your loved one.* My suggestion is to work with officiants who use a questionnaire to gather information about you or your loved one.

Guest Speakers & Family Traditions

Note to leader: You can open this conversation with a comment such as: "Think back to a funeral or memorial you attended. Were the guest speakers engaging, and did each have a unique perspective of the deceased?"

Guest speakers often tend to be individuals who have shared a similar background with the deceased. Instead, choose speakers from different parts of your life to offer unique perspectives of you, creating variety in the stories shared.

> Question: Who in your background would you select to have a good variety of speakers?

For example:

- A family member
- A coworker
- A schoolmate
- A mentor
- A neighbor
- A house of worship member or leader
- A fellow volunteer at a charitable nonprofit

Note to leader: Ask your group to give examples of what they believe are family or organizational traditions. Examples below.

Question: If you were to include a family or organizational tradition at the service, what would it be and why?

An example of this could be bell ringing, which is common for first responders. It might be military honors with a rifle volley (where it is practical and appropriate, such as at a public or national cemetery), then the playing of taps followed by flag folding and presentation of the flag to a survivor. Or perhaps the singing of a particular hymn or prayer meaningful to the family.

Death Notifications

Question: When you lost a loved one, how were you notified? How did you feel about the form of communication used?

Note to leader: Communicating that an anticipated death will occur soon benefits family, friends, and your loved one's coworkers by giving them advance notice, allowing them more time to process their emotional reaction, make travel plans, or request time off.

Each family will have to decide whether social media is an appropriate means of communication. Using your loved one's social media account will distribute the news to his/her friends. It can be highly effective, but out of respect for family members and key friends, a phone call may be the most appropriate before an email is sent or an announcement posted on social media.

Note: Using your loved one's social media account will distribute the news to his/her friends, which should provide more coverage than just using *your* friends list.

Note to leader: There are two scenarios to discuss with your group. Review the Anticipated Death Letter and Sudden Death Letter templates (p. 99 and 101 in the workbook) for their reaction.

ASSIGNMENTS

Make a list of your service and reception needs to prepare for an interview with each venue's representative. Then, during the interview, ask if each need can be met and at what cost. Also ask for a list of recommended officiants and call them to begin communication. Ask the officiants you interview how they *obtain* information about you, or if at-need, how they *capture information* about your loved one.

If you wish to include pictures, videos, or music in your service, gather your media files and ask someone to prepare a presentation for you (or you can do it yourself). Too much media will go long and lose the attention of the attendees. Just enough media highlights the deceased without making these elements the focus of the service. It's like salt; a little can go a long way, so just enough enhances the service.

If you are a pre-planner, draft a list of family members and friends that you want your survivors to call for a personal death notification. Making that list now—and with current phone numbers—will help your survivors through this highly emotional task. Draft a death notification letter they can use for social media, should they choose.

CHAPTER TEN

UNDERSTANDING YOUR HEALTH INSURANCE

GOAL OF THE CHAPTER

Chapter 10 will help you understand your medical insurance plan so you can work within the parameters of your provider's coverage to ensure you will get the help you need without unanticipated costs. You will learn how to scrutinize and choose a plan, stay within your plan, and how survivors can chronicle expenses while their loved one is in the hospital.

MAIN POINTS

- There are different kinds of health plans available—a Preferred Provider Organization (PPO) or a Health Maintenance Organization (HMO).
- A health insurance plan will not cover "out-of-network" costs (treatment, doctor fees, medical equipment) without authorization. Make sure to stay "in-network" or immediately request authorization so you won't be charged for the entire bill.

- It's important to explore exactly what is covered "in-network" in your plan—such as necessary medical equipment or specialists.
- Having a system to chronicle your loved one's medical treatments, doctor visits, specialist visits, and other related billable services while in the hospital can provide you with documentation should your billing be questionable.

DISCUSSION POINTS

Understanding Your Health Plan

Question: Do you have an HMO or PPO? Have you taken the time to investigate your plan to see what *is* and *is not* covered? Why is this important?

Answer: Because an insured person may assume that a treatment or drug is covered, only to find out at the time of treatment or purchase that it is not covered.

Note to leader: This is both a fact and point of interest that needs to be shared with your group.

Going outside of your plan could result in being denied reimbursement when submitting the bill. Review the scenario in *When It's Time®* on pages 143–144. As an example, someone covered through an HMO who decides to go outside of their plan to receive treatment that is not life threatening at a local medical facility or hospital could be responsible for 100 percent of the bill.

Note: If you are required to go out-of-network due to an emergency, call your HMO to advise them of the need and out-of-network facility, then request authorization. Make sure to record the HMO representative's name and gain approval for your emergency.

Point of interest: When people change plans without inspecting and evaluating their new plan, they may not receive the same benefits and convenience to which they were accustomed. The new medical plan may not serve them well when considering their residential location and the lack of services provided at their new medical facility. For example, if a person has an HMO, the closest medical facility could be a three-to-four-hour drive. HMOs typically do not let you go out-of-network just for convenience.

Point of interest: If you will be traveling, I advise you to consider purchasing medical travel insurance before leaving on a trip out of the state or country. Travel medical insurance is an excellent option to ensure that you are covered for your medical needs rather than guessing and hoping.

Tracking Treatment

Question: Has anyone developed a system of recording all of the activity that takes place in the hospital room and then comparing it to the bills you received? What pieces of information do you include? Why is it important to record this information?

Answer: If you or a family member is hospitalized, when you receive the bills—which can come in weeks later—it's doubtful you'll recall every doctor's visit, treatment provided, lab work ordered, durable equipment used, etc. With so many moving parts during one's hospital stay, mistakes happen and the bill may have discrepancies in the charges. It is the responsibility of the patient and family to record the activity and then compare it to the bills for accuracy. Anytime you or your family member receive medical care, it's a good idea to record the following information:

- Doctor visits: Doctor's name, date, time of visit.
- Medication given: Name of drug and who administered the drug.
- Lab work ordered and what specifically the order was for.
- Durable equipment used (e.g., breathing machine, dialysis, etc.).

- Physical therapy: Name of therapist, date, and time.
- Meals: Date and time.

After reviewing your bills and comparing the details of the bills with your records, if there are discrepancies, call your hospital and have a conversation revealing your records versus the bill. If the discrepancies are significant, and if you do not find a workable solution with the billing department, consider calling your insurance company and asking them to connect with the hospital/medical facility's billing department to begin their negotiations. With significant billing discrepancies, your insurance company has agents who will pursue this aggressively for a workable agreement, which could save you thousands of dollars.

ASSIGNMENTS

If you have not reviewed your health insurance plan, review specifically for items they do not cover, or what is considered out-of-network. Brainstorm a list of hypothetical treatments that might be relevant to you. For example: "If I want spots removed from my skin because I don't like the way they make me look, am I covered?" You will likely receive an answer similar to, "Yes, we do that procedure, but we do not cover the cost if not prescribed by your physician; therefore, you are one-hundred percent responsible for the payment." Call your HMO and contact a representative to get the answers you need. Other good questions to ask include: "If I have an emergency and either my family or an emergency medical technician transports me to an out-of-network provider, am I covered?" and "How do I inform you, as my provider, that this scenario is happening or has happened? What should I expect?"

If you have a mobile phone, enter your HMO's direct line to call for approval for an out-of-network emergency treatment.

If you are out of your state of residence or country, call your HMO before leaving your immediate geographical area and inquire how your provider recommends you receive medical treatment while out of their defined area.

CHAPTER ELEVEN

APPLYING FOR VETERAN BENEFITS

GOAL OF THE CHAPTER

Veterans have burial benefits for any of the national cemeteries, including Arlington, but only if you are a registered veteran. For burial in a public or private cemetery, you may be eligible for veterans' burial allowances if you're paying for the burial and funeral costs and you won't be reimbursed by any other organization, such as another government agency or the veteran's employer. This chapter explains how to sign up as a veteran, who can sign up for you if you are deceased, and what the Veterans Affairs office (VA) will supply at a national cemetery or Arlington.

MAIN POINTS

- All veterans must register before receiving any earned benefits. Start at your local County Veteran Service Office (CVSO) with your Veterans Benefit Counselor (VBC).
- The VA offers a burial allowance to cover the

costs of a funeral, burial in a national cemetery, the plot (gravesite) or interment, and transporting the remains. Certain family members and professionals can apply for these benefits on behalf of the veteran.

- Veterans who meet certain requirements are eligible for military funeral honors, memorial marker or headstone, and burial flags.

DISCUSSION POINTS

Veteran Registration

Question: If you are a US veteran, in which branch did you serve? What was your job and rank in that branch? Where were you based?

Most importantly, thank you for serving our nation, we are grateful!

Question: If you are a veteran, have you registered at our local CVSO? If so, how was that experience?

Point of interest: Burial benefits for veterans are easy to apply for and receive. The VBC offers a once-per-month seminar, and all veterans and family members are invited to learn about earned benefits. For active-duty service men/women, it is difficult to define in this book because the benefits are based on the cause of death, and sometimes the place death occurred. I encourage survivors of active-duty service men/women to either contact the base chaplain or administrator or their local VBC for more information.

Point of interest: A veteran's spouse can be buried at a national cemetery or Arlington as a veteran benefit. Attending one of the monthly seminars at your local CVSO or by phoning your VBC, you will learn how to apply and other pertinent information.

Point of interest: To register as a veteran at your local CVSO, you will need the following documents:

- Your DD214 form (discharge, or separation paperwork)
- Your marriage license and, if applicable, divorce paperwork
- Your marital history on both sides of your family
- Your banking information for direct deposits

Note to leader: The following question is bound to open up discussion. You can either let it take its course or keep the group on track by saying, "Your local Veterans Benefit Counselor's sole purpose is to help veterans and can provide more information on this subject."

Question: If you experienced an injury, medical issue, or disability as a result of your service, have you considered filing a claim for compensation?

The *When It's Time®* book tells a story of a veteran who was suffering from Agent Orange exposure and was told by friends, both civilian and military veterans, that he would not qualify for compensation. But through his VBC, he applied for and received over $500,000 in compensation. I cannot emphasize enough the importance of you learning more about burial benefits and financial compensation if you qualify for an injury or prolonged medical diagnosis for both your benefit and your survivors. This begins with an appointment at our local CVSO with the VBC. Please, do it today!

Burial Benefits

Point of interest: To file for burial benefits, you first need to register as a veteran. If you are a survivor and your loved one did not register prior to their death, then the following people can apply for burial benefits:

- Surviving spouse
- Surviving partner from a legal union
- Surviving child of the veteran
- Partner of a veteran
- Executor of the veteran's estate

Question: If you are a veteran, where would you like to be buried? At a local cemetery, a national cemetery, or Arlington? Why?

Point of interest: There can be limitations at a national cemetery or Arlington, such as the wait time, length of a service, and what is provided, but the grounds are beautiful and will remain that way versus a public or private cemetery, which may not be as well maintained.

At a national cemetery, you will have:

- A service time limited to 30 minutes, versus a funeral home or church where a service could go on for hours.
- A service held in an outdoor shelter (a three-sided structure with a roof), which will have some exposure to the elements (temperature).
- A service paid for by the government, which includes the cost of the shelter, plot/vault, marker (headstone or flat marker), military honors, cemetery staff, and possibly transportation of the remains (check with your local VBC to ensure this is true at your time of need).

If you are applying for burial at Arlington, you can expect up to a one-year waiting period. This is true for both burial with a casket or cremated remains. The exceptions are first, active-duty personnel who died from hostile wounds, and second, those who are active-duty but did not die from hostile wounds.

Question: Has anyone in our group had a family member who was a veteran buried at a public or private cemetery? If so, what VA financial benefits were applied to their burial costs? How did your family apply for these benefits?

Military Honors

Question: Has anyone in our group attended a military funeral, either at a national, public, or private cemetery? What do you recall about the military honors at the service?

Point of interest: If military honors are what you would like at your service, your funeral home/mortuary of choice will arrange this for you if you make the request. To obtain the flag, you need your DD214 form and a death certificate. Upon providing the documentation, your local US Postal Service will provide the flag, regardless of where the service will be held. On occasion, your funeral home/mortuary will provide the flag.

ASSIGNMENTS

If you are a US veteran and you have not registered at your local CVSO, make an appointment with a VBC or attend a monthly seminar to learn about the benefits you have earned. If you cannot locate your DD214 form, your local VBC can help you apply for a new one.

Take a trip to visit your local national cemetery or the cemeteries you are considering for yourself or a family member. If you are a US veteran, have you made a decision to be buried at a national cemetery? If not, why not? If you are pre-planning and choose a public or private cemetery, take the necessary steps to apply for benefits earned to offset the cost.

If you intend to have a military marker, draft your inscription and share with your family. Making choices as a pre-planner about your funeral/memorial service in the future includes either you or survivors choosing what will be inscribed on your marker.

CHAPTER 12

ASSESSING SOCIAL SECURITY BENEFITS

GOAL OF THE CHAPTER

The Social Security Administration (SSA) was designed to serve you, the taxpayer, although maneuvering the system might make you wonder if that is the case! This chapter will walk you through qualification, application, and expectations for the program, which includes benefits such as retirement income, support for people who are disabled, survivors of workers who have died, dependents of beneficiaries, and more.

MAIN POINTS

- Qualification for SSA benefits is based on credits, which are calculated by your income.
- The one-time lump-sum death benefit provides a small amount for burial costs.
- Social Security Disability Insurance (SSDI) and Supplemental Security Income (SSI) are different programs with different qualification criteria. It is helpful to consult an attorney before applying for SSDI or SSI.

- Spouse SSA survivor benefits can be generous. Consider implications before remarrying.

DISCUSSION POINTS

Qualification

Point of interest: The standard qualification for a person to earn benefits from SSA is by earning credits. Credits are calculated by your income and the longevity of your income.

> Question: If you are not already retired, do you know your total credits earned? If so, how did you find this information? Were you surprised by the number of credits you have earned, or have not earned? Why?

Answer: The SSA website has this available if you log on and create an account. Who has completed this already? How difficult was it? It's a good idea to check your account yearly on the SSA website to ensure your earnings are reported accurately because mistakes will impact your financial benefit when you apply.

Point of interest: To qualify for SSA benefits, you must earn forty credits or be a qualifying survivor/ dependent that is granted the decedent's benefits. For every $1,470 earned you will be granted a credit, and up to four credits per year can be achieved as of the writing of this leader's guide. The more you earn, the more you pay into SSA; therefore, the more you will receive when you retire and apply for this benefit.

Benefits

Question: Has anyone here heard of or applied for the one-time lump-sum death benefit? How long did it take from the time of application until received?

Point of interest: In the 1930s, a law was passed that allowed money to be paid out as a one-time sum to survivors for the burial of their loved one. To this day it is still called the lump-sum death benefit. That number was low then and it has not risen much over the last eight decades. As of the writing of this leader's guide, the one-time-death benefit is $255.

Question: Can anyone articulate the difference between Social Security Disability Insurance and Supplemental Security Income?"

Note to leader: It is common that few will be able to articulate the difference.

Answer: SSDI is available to workers who qualify with 40-earned credits, meaning they have paid into SSA's trust fund called FICA Social Security Tax. SSDI is paid through payroll taxes. SSI is a program offering disability benefits to low-income qualified individuals who do not meet the criteria for earning the necessary work credits for SSDI or do not have an income history. SSI is paid through general taxes, which do not come from the same SSA trust fund.

Note to leader: This section is especially important if you have group members who question their qualification for either SSDI or SSI.

"As a group, let's read what the qualification criteria is for each in When It's Time® found on pages 169–171." The reason for reading it together is so you can highlight specifics that may interest you or a family member. Then direct group members to the SSA websites listed in the book to address specific topics.

Question: Why do you think a common saying is: "Before you apply for SSDI or SSI, contact an attorney?" Does anyone know a person who had hired an attorney for this process? What was the outcome?

Answer: It is common to be rejected the first, second, and even third time before you qualify. So how can an attorney help you?

- The attorney will better understand whether or not you have a valid claim.
- The attorney will better understand the process so you stay within the guidelines and enhance your potential for approval.

It is possible that your local SSA office may respect that you have an attorney who knows how to work within the system; hence, a higher percentage of your benefit will be approved.

Question: Has anyone examined or received survivor benefits, such as medical insurance, education expenses for people who qualify? What did you learn through this process?

Note to leader: Survivor benefits through SSA can be generous. Researching these benefits can be of immense value to you.

Point of interest: If you have experienced a loss of your spouse, you can be entitled to receive the larger of the two financial retirement incomes (yours or your spouses), but there is a catch. If you remarry before receiving your spouse's larger financial retirement income, you may forfeit this benefit and be awarded only your earned benefit, which is smaller. It is wise to check with your SSA office before considering remarrying if this could be an issue for you.

ASSIGNMENTS

If you have not begun receiving your financial retirement benefit from the SSA, go online and create an account. Then review the data under your name/social security number for accuracy. Specifically, look at your credits earned and your income earned, dating as far back as you have records to validate the accuracy. Remember, your income retirement from SSA is based on their records, so if you find a reason to request a review, gather your documentation and present your case.

If you qualify for the lump-sum death benefit but have not applied for the payout, call your SSA office and ask if there is an expiration date for this payout.

If you qualify for SSDI or SSI but have been turned down, consider calling an attorney who specializes in SSA. The one-time investment for the attorney fee could help you qualify for one of the benefits.

If you are the guardians of a minor whose parents have passed away, research the SSA benefits they could qualify for, such as financial aid for education, medical benefits, income, and more.

If you have questions or are ready to apply for SSA benefits, make an appointment with a representative. Before your appointment, review the list of questions on page 172 of *When It's Time*® and add your own based on your life dynamics. Remember, there are no bad questions, only questions that are not asked and answered, leaving you in a position to lose benefits that you have earned.

CHAPTER THIRTEEN

GRIEVING YOUR LOSS

GOAL OF THE CHAPTER

When a loved one dies, responses to the loss vary greatly. There can be tremendous emotional pain, prolonged grief, grief postponed, guilt, relief, total confusion, and a litany of other responses. All are normal, but not necessarily healthy. How can you emotionally prepare for an anticipated death? And when death occurs, how do you step into grief and mourning in a healthy way? This chapter guides you through emotional recovery and building a team to assist you in every step of the grief process.

MAIN POINTS

- Grieving is an inevitable part of life. It's not *if* we will experience it, but *when*.
- When facing an imminent death of a loved one, contact *your* doctor for a checkup and conversation about both your health.
- Grief responses can be physical, emotional, and psychological, and people process grief in different ways.

- The "ministry of presence" is one of the best ways to support the bereaved.
- Building and activating your team will help you delegate tasks so they can support you.

DISCUSSION POINTS

Symptoms of Grief

Point of interest: Death is a normal part of the life cycle. But, unlike a birth, which is celebrated, the death of a loved one can be debilitating for survivors. When relationships have been difficult due to decisions made and consequences suffered, the loss of that family member or friend can be emotionally heightened, or at minimum, be extremely difficult to process and accept.

Note to leader: Before starting the discussion, review with your group the stages of grief (book p. 179). Death is a normal part of the life cycle, but it can still be debilitating for survivors. Acknowledging your grief, understanding the grief stages, and working through your grief—not around your grief—will assist you in your recovery.

Question: Who within our group has experienced the pain of a loss, anticipated or otherwise? Who did you lose? What symptoms of grief did you experience and how did you address them?

Grief takes a toll. When the death of a loved one is imminent, a soon-to-be survivor should meet with their doctor for both a physical and emotional checkup. Inform your doctor about the imminent death so your medical history will include this in your records should you need medication for anxiety or a referral to a therapist now or in the future. You will be considered a priority patient. Why is this important? Because the bereaved can put their own medical conditions and wellbeing on hold. Staying healthy for your living loved ones and for your own healing is a priority.

Note to leader: Use the information about the five givens (book p.177) below as a setup for the questions that follow.

Preparing for an imminent death and understanding loss can help you process through the reality of life. The majority of us will face grief and mourning one day. In the book titled *The Five Things We Cannot Change* by Dr. David Richo, it says:

- Everything changes and ends.
- Things do not always go according to plan.
- Life is not always fair.
- Pain is part of life.
- People are not loving and loyal all the time.

There is a harsh reality to the *five givens*, but too often we choose to ignore these facts; therefore, our reality is distorted. Is grief painful? Absolutely! Can it be debilitating? Without a doubt, yes!

Question: For people who have experienced either an imminent death or sudden death, describe the process you went through. When did you feel that your recovery was well on its way?

Question: As a group, if you have experienced more than one loss, did you learn from the past and apply what you learned to the next loss? Did this help your recovery from the second loss? Describe why or why not?

The Ministry of Presence

Note to leader: Review what the "ministry of presence" means (book pp.184–186). When a person is anticipating the death of a loved one or recovering from the loss, having someone who will "just listen and not try to analyze or fix you" offers a vehicle for expression, comfort, and at times, a safe place to express their anger. This person should be a trusted friend or family member who will:

- *Keep the conversations confidential.*
- *Be available when the grieving person needs to talk.*
- *Focus on the grieving person and not themselves.*
- *Be a listener, not a talker.*
- *Be available for the short- and long-term position.*

- *Wait for the grieving person to ask their opinion, rather than offer it.*
- *Expect nothing in return because they are there to serve, not be served.*

Question: Have you had a person in your life fill this role when you were grieving, and what was your experience? When you consider a loss in your life, who did you turn to for help and why them?

Tapping Your Team

Point of interest: When there is a sudden loss, any pre-planning your loved one completed is now activated. However, as survivors, this process can put tremendous pressure on you. Having a team help you during this process offers comfort and efficiency through sharing the administrative tasks. We were never designed to "do it on our own," but rather, we are designed to be in relationships—healthy relationships. During our time of need, having dependable, trusted friends is a gift. There is a proverb found in the Hebrew Scriptures (a.k.a. the Old Testament) that describes a type of friend. It says, ". . . there is a friend who sticks closer than a brother" (Proverbs 18:24).

e to leader: Have your group examine the team diagram the workbook on page 12 and discuss what roles each would play in an end-of-life scenario. Just accumulating names for tasks is not the goal here. The goal is to recruit the right people with the right hearts, knowing what they are capable of accomplishing.

> Question: If you experienced a loss, how did having or not having a team in place affect your grief experience?

Note to leader: The "blessing of delegation" works two ways when you have team members on your grief journey. First, you (or your team leader) can delegate tasks to be done to lighten your burden. Secondly, your team members have agreed to their role, so blessing them with tasks to do encourages them because they are helping you, and that empowers them to do even more.

As you build your team, you may find that people you thought would be dedicated supporters actually shy away from you, stepping back rather than forward. When this happens—and it will—don't be offended because people respond differently to death and grief. Our American culture does not always do well in this area.

The value of having a team established before a death occurs cannot be measured with a matrix. When you consider the emotions involved in grief sharing, the bonding that happens, and the personal and spiritual growth everyone will experience, it's undeniable that this could be one of the greatest acts of love you will be part of.

Question: If you are a survivor, how did you know/decide when you were ready to start taking back tasks that had been delegated to your team?

ASSIGNMENTS

Draft a list of people you'd like to ask to be part of your team and start calling or meeting with them to discuss their role.

Once your team has been assembled, identify who the leaders will be and decide what you want to do yourself. Managing a team is work in itself, and it can be helpful to have a few key team leaders to help you delegate. Keep in mind that your plan may need modification when what you thought you could do hypothetically doesn't match what you are able to do in reality.

Start a list of household tasks that you could delegate when the time arises.

APPENDIX A

SURVIVOR CHECKLIST©

Of all the tools and suggestions in the leader's guide, the Survivor Checklist© may be the most useful. The goal of the checklist is to assist survivors with every step—from death to grieving to recovery. By helping you develop a team, the Survivor Checklist© will assist you long after your loss, teaching you how to stay administratively strong.

Note to leader: Encourage your group to independently study the Survivor Checklist©. It is designed to assist survivors on a daily, weekly and monthly basis as both a reminder of key legal and personal things to accomplish, and to ask for help. It will also assist the pre-planner in focusing on legal and personal matters to accomplish, assisting their survivors at their time of need.

AFTERWORD

NOW IT'S TIME!

Congratulations! You have spent weeks leading your group to be educated pre-planners! You have also assisted people on their journey as survivors, or at minimum, prepared them to be survivors. What you have accomplished as a qualified leader will only be truly recognized and appreciated as your group members put their plans into practice. You may hear from them thanking you for your time invested, but whether you hear from them or not, please know that your gift to them is valuable. I encourage you to assemble another group and offer the same expertise you displayed, leaving them with the same gift: knowledge of how to pre-plan and recover as a survivor!

Where do you and your group members go from here? In chapter two, I commented on having a Trust written and posed the question:

> "Have you moved your assets into the Trust, so they are protected?"

Without that final step, the Trust will not serve purpose. The same principle applies to your overall plan. I strongly encourage you to finish what you have started for everyone's benefit.

A good illustration of not finishing the job is my story about landscaping our backyard with plants one year ago. We installed a drip system so the plants could thrive with life-giving water. After installing the new system, I realized later that I needed to install more drip emitters for full coverage. I put it off for weeks, maybe even months, before I finally took the time to finish the job. The downside was these plants did not survive because I procrastinated rather than completing the job. Please don't be me when it comes to your plan. I learned a valuable lesson!

To help you complete your plan, I offer downloadable resources on the *When It's Time®* website, https://whenitstime.org/. There you'll find the *When It's Time®* Group Reflection Survey© and "Expectations You Can Have for Yourself in Grief" by Dr. Therese A. Rondo. You can also subscribe to the email list to receive the Pre-Planning Funeral/Memorial Questionnaire©.

(Scan and scroll to end of webpage.)

May the Lord give you peace and grace as you finalize your pre-planning, and shower you survivors with love, direction, and a restored heart. I know it can happen because I am a recipient of His mercy.

Made in the USA
Columbia, SC
27 November 2024

47254752R00072